GW00738326

HODDER HOME LEARNING

General Knowledge

AGE 9-11

Boswell Taylor

As a parent, you can play a major role in your child's education by your interest and encouragement. This book is designed to help your child to acquire a good general knowledge, and to develop an enthusiasm for learning.

Each double page consists of a single test. The left-hand page presents multiple choice questions with three options for each question. On the right-hand page, the questions are open-ended and more difficult. Answers should be written on the dotted lines. On each double page there is also a time test to be written on a separate piece of paper. Answers to all questions are provided at the back of the book.

Over the page you will find advice on how to help your child to get the most out of this book.

Hodder Children's Books

NATIONAL CONFEDERATION OF PARENT TEACHER ASSOCIATIONS

NCPTA

The only home learning programme supported by the NCPTA

How to help your child

- Encourage your child to ask questions. Answer them as fully as you can, but never be afraid to say that you don't know. Suggest that you find out the answer together.

- Try to build up a small reference library at home, starting with an encyclopaedia and a dictionary.

- Encourage your child to use the reference section of your local library. Go along with your child if you can and explore the books together.

- Help your child to develop important research skills by showing how to use the contents list and index to find the information he or she needs.

- Make sure that finding out is fun – children learn best if they are enjoying themselves!

Published by Hodder Children's Books 1995

10 9 8 7 6 5 4 3

ISBN 0 340 65112 1

Copyright © Boswell Taylor 1982

The right of Boswell Taylor to be identified as the author of the Work has been asserted by him in accordance with the Copyright, Designs and Patents Act 1988.

Printed and bound in Great Britain

Hodder Children's Books
A division of Hodder Headline plc
338 Euston Road
London NW1 3BH

Previously published as Test Your Child's General Knowledge

To begin with …

Here are three questions, below which are the three possible answers from which you have to choose.

What are the places called where the following animals are kept?

1 pigs ....   2 sheep ....   3 horses ....

a stable   b sty   c fold

Show which answer goes with each question, like this:

1 pigs ....*b*........   2 sheep ....*c*........   3 horses ....*a*........

Now test yourself with these:

What sounds are made by the following animals?

4 turkey ....   5 cow ....   6 pig ....

a grunts   b moos   c gobbles

What names are given to the places used in the following sports?

7 tennis ....   8 boxing ....   9 cricket ....

a ring   b pitch   c court

When a question is asked like this:

1 Which is the largest ocean in the world?   ....

write the answer on the dotted line, like this:

1 Which is the largest ocean in the world?   *Pacific*
....

Now do these:

2 Whose official home is 10 Downing Street?   ....

3 How many strings does a violin have?   ....

4 Of which country is the Great Barrier Reef a part?   ....

5 What do we call a person who flies an aircraft?   ....

Medley 1

What are the sounds made by the following animals?

1 cat ....   2 dog ....   3 horse ....
  a neighs   b barks   c purrs

What are the usual contents of the following?

4 kettle ....   5 purse ....   6 wardrobe ....
  a clothes   b water   c money

What special names are given to the places where

7 grain is ground? ....   8 fruit trees grow?..........   9 plays are shown?..........
  a orchard   b mill   c theatre

Which fictional characters are linked with the following?

10 'Open Sesame' .... 11 a glass slipper .... 12 an old lamp ....
  a Aladdin   b Cinderella   c Ali Baba

Who are the Roman goddesses of the following?

13 hunting .... 14 love ....   15 wisdom ....
  a Venus   b Diana   c Minerva

In what countries are the following found?

16 the Pyramids .... 17 the Blarney Stone .... 18 the Wailing Wall ....
  a Irish Republic   b Israel   c Egypt

In which countries are these mountains?

19 Ararat .... 20 Cotopaxi .... 21 Cook ....
  a New Zealand   b Ecuador   c Turkey

Of what organizations are the following the headquarters?

22 Scotland Yard .... 23 Vatican .... 24 Pentagon ....
  a London Police   b US Defence   c Roman Catholic Church

What are measured by the following?

25 the cran .... 26 knots .... 27 hands ....
  a fish   b height of horse   c a ship's speed

What single words can be used for the following?

28 so let it be .... 29 higher still .... 30 'I have found it!' ....
  a eureka   b amen   c excelsior

31 According to the rhyme what kind of meat did Jack Sprat eat? ....

32 What do we call the yellow part of an egg? ....

33 What was the ship on which Nelson died? ....

34 Sour milk consists of curds and what else? ....

35 Where is the rattlesnake's rattle? ....

36 What tree gives us the acorn? ....

37 What relation to you is your mother's father? ....

38 Whose knights sat at the Round Table? ....

39 What flower is the national emblem of England? ....

40 By what name are the Yeomen of the Guard at the Tower of London better known? ....

41 How many sides has an octagon? ....

42 Where in your body is your 'funny bone'? ....

43 How many dwarfs helped Snow White? ....

44 How many playing cards are there in an ordinary pack? ....

45 How many men did a Roman centurion command? ....

Time Test

How many can you write down in the given time?
On a separate sheet of paper make three columns:

Fish   **Girls' Names**   **Islands**

Write the names you know. Have your list checked.
Count 2 for each correct answer. Check your rating.

Time allowed: 9 and 10 year olds – 2 minutes
11 year olds and over – 1 minute

People

Who would be likely to use the following?

1 plough ....   2 saw ....   3 telescope ....
a astronomer   b farmer   c carpenter

What do we call the chief persons connected with the following?

4 army ....   5 newspaper ....   6 ship ....
a editor   b captain   c general

Who worships in these kinds of buildings?

7 synagogue ....   8 mosque ....   9 church ....
a Christian   b Muslim   c Jew

What do we call the chief persons who sell the following?

10 vegetables ....   11 writing paper ....   12 tools ....
a greengrocer   b ironmonger   c stationer

What animals are associated with the following?

13 Father Christmas ....   14 Dick Whittington ....   15 Dick Turpin ....
a cat   b horse   c reindeer

Who are the patron saints of these countries?

16 Scotland ....   17 Ireland ....   18 Wales ....
a St David   b St Patrick   c St Andrew

What important people live at these residences?

19 Windsor Castle ....   20 The Vatican ....   21 The White House ....
a The Pope   b British sovereign   c US president

What special feats made these people 'famous firsts'?

22 Edmund Hillary ....   23 Neil Armstrong ....   24 Yuri Gagarin ....
a travelled in space   b climbed Everest   c landed on the Moon

With what inventions are these persons associated?

25 Alexander G. Bell ....   26 James Watt ....   27 Wright brothers ....
a steam engine   b telephone   c aeroplane

Who founded these organizations?

28 Salvation Army ....   29 Scouts ....   30 Red Cross ....
a Jean H. Dunant   b William Booth   c Lord Baden-Powell

31 Of what country was Cleopatra queen? ....

32 Who was the apostle who betrayed Jesus? ....

33 Who founded the Muslim faith? ....

34 Who first brought tobacco to Britain? ....

35 What title was given to the German Emperors? ....

36 Which president of the United States was a film actor? ....

37 Which Soviet leader introduced the policies of glasnost and perestroika to the then USSR? ....

38 Who was the Russian who wrote *War and Peace?* ....

39 Who was the first woman to fly in space? ....

40 Who was the first woman Speaker in the House of Commons? ....

41 Which surgeon made the first heart transplant? ....

42 In which country was Kylie Minogue born? ....

43 Who was the first woman Prime Minister of Britain? ....

44 Who was the father of Queen Elizabeth II? ....

45 Which national leader was famous for his 'Book of Thoughts'? ....

Time Test

How many can you write down in the given time?
On a separate sheet of paper make three columns:

Footballers   **Painters**   **Inventors**

Write the names you know. Have your list checked.
Count 2 for each correct answer. Check your rating.

Time allowed: 9 and 10 year olds – 2 minutes
                         11 year olds and over – 1 minute

Food and Drink

What foods do we associate with the following?

1 Shrove Tuesday .... 2 Good Friday .... 3 Christmas Day ....
a mince pies   b pancakes   c hot cross buns

Which animals supply the following?

4 venison ....   5 pork ....   6 beef ....
a pigs   b bullocks   c deer

What kinds of food and drink have these place names?

7 Brussels ....   8 Burgundy ....   9 Stilton ....
a vegetable   b cheese   c wine

What are the main ingredients of these foods?

10 toad-in-the-hole   11 Welsh rarebit   12 angels-on-horseback

....
  a oysters   b sausages   c cheese

For which food are the following countries noted?

13 Turkey ....   14 France ....   15 Italy ....
  a pizza   b kebab   c snails

From which countries do these cheeses come?

16 Edam ....   17 Gorgonzola .... 18 Brie ....
  a Holland   b Italy   c France

To which fruits do the following names refer?

19 Jaffa ....   20 Conference ....   21 Victoria ....
  a plum   b pear   c orange

Which of these vegetables grow in the following ways?

22 under the ground .... 23 on the ground .... 24 on stems ....
  a broad beans   b carrot   c marrow

What drinks are made from the following?

25 malt and hops .... 26 apples .... 27 molasses ....
  a cider   b rum   c beer

What kinds of foods are the following?

28 cutlet ....   29 ketchup ....   30 cheddar ....
  a meat   b cheese   c sauce

31 What is grown in fields called paddies? ....

32 Are anchovies vegetables or fish? ....

33 What fish may become a kipper or a bloater? ....

34 What sauce is traditionally served with roast lamb? ....

35 What kind of pastry is used in making éclairs? ....

36 What do the seeds of the cacao tree make? ....

37 What fruit is generally used to make marmalade? ....

38 What is porridge usually made from? ....

39 What kind of meat provides sirloin? ....

40 What is the insect that gives us honey? ....

41 What beverage comes from China, Sri Lanka and India?.............................

42 What is butter produced from? ....

43 What kind of tree or bush supplies blackberries? ....

44 What is yoghurt made from? ....

45 What part of the plant is used to make mustard? ....

Time Test

How many can you write down in the given time?
On a separate sheet of paper make three columns:

Drinks   **Vegetables**   **Fruits**

Write the names you know. Have your list checked.
Count 2 for each correct answer. Check your rating.

Time allowed: 9 and 10 year olds – 2 minutes
                  11 year olds and over – 1 minute

Medley 2

In nursery rhymes what numbers apply to the following?

1 miles to Babylon	2 bags of wool	3 Duke of York's men .....
a 3	b 70	c 10,000

What names are given to the young of the following?

4 hare	5 swan	6 deer ....
a fawn	b leveret	c cygnet

What names are given to the people at the following?

7 concert	8 church service	9 art gallery ....
a viewers	b audience	c congregation

What kinds of animals in stories are the following?

10 Tarka	11 Eeyore	12 Captain Flint ....
a donkey	b parrot	c otter

Where are the following important places?

13 Red Square	14 Forbidden City.............	15 St Peter's Square ....
a Moscow (Russia)	b Rome (Italy)	c Beijing (China)

Which Biblical people were known for the following?

16 strength	17 patience	18 wisdom ....
a Solomon	b Samson	c Job

What are damaged or polluted by the following?

19 aerosols	20 acid rain	21 nitrates ....
a water	b ozone layer	c rainforests

Where are the following found?

22 pampas	23 tundra	24 the Rand ....
a South Africa	b North Russia	c South America

Which creatures in myths had the following unusual features?

25 two faces	26 three heads	27 one eye ....
a the Cyclops	b Janus	c Cerberus

What did each of the following devise?

28 Isaac Pitman	29 Admiral Beaufort.......	30 John Curwen ....
a wind force scale	b tonic sol-fa	c shorthand

31 Of what word is 'fridge' the shortened form? ....

32 Which is the longest river in the world? ....

33 Who was the leader of the 'Merry Men' of Sherwood Forest? ....

34 How many years are there in a decade? ....

35 What capital city is divided by the river Danube? ....

36 In English cricket how many balls are bowled in a normal over? ....

37 What is the rope that a cowboy uses called? ....

38 What is the name given to a foot specialist? ....

39 What colour is the cornflower? ....

40 What colour are babies' eyes at birth? ....

41 What woman's name is linked with waxworks? ....

42 What is the colour of a sapphire? ....

43 What is a puffin? ....

44 Where does lava come from? ....

45 What country has the word 'Suomi' on its stamps? ....

Time Test

How many can you write down in the given time?
On a separate sheet of paper make three columns:

Clothes   **Countries**   **Tools**

Write the names you know. Have your list checked.
Count 2 for each correct answer. Check your rating.

Time allowed: 9 and 10 year olds – 2 minutes
                   11 year olds and over – 1 minute

Science and Machines

What do the following measure?

1 metre .... 2 second .... 3 litre ....
a liquid   b length   c time

Where are these instruments likely to be found?

4 telescope .... 5 speedometer .... 6 metronome ....
a in a music room   b in an observatory   c in a motor car

Who would be most likely to use these tools in the course of their work?

7 hoe .... 8 chisel .... 9 scissors ....
a gardener   b hairdresser   c carpenter

What are studied in these subjects?

10 geology .... 11 zoology .... 12 botany ....
a animals   b flowers   c rocks

What do you associate these substances with?

13 fluoride .... 14 yeast .... 15 mercury ....
a bread   b toothpaste   c thermometers

Which of the planets are the following?

16 the largest .... 17 nearest to the sun..... 18 the smallest................
a Jupiter   b Mercury   c Pluto

What elements are used in the following?

19 wire .... 20 coins .... 21 lamps ....
a neon   b copper   c nickel

Who invented the following?

22 ball-point pen   23 pneumatic   24 safety-razor
                     bicycle tyre
    ....
a Dunlop   b Biro   c Gillette

In which parts of your body are the following?

25 ribs .... 26 skull .... 27 shin ....
a head   b chest   c leg

Who discovered the following?

28 vaccination.................. 29 penicillin .... 30 radium ....
a Alexander Fleming   b Marie Curie   c Dr Edward Jenner

31 What is coal made of? ....

32 At what temperature on the Centigrade
thermometer does water boil? ....

33 At what temperature on the Centigrade
thermometer does water turn to ice? ....

34 What is the machine that takes photographs called? ....

35 What does a sundial measure? ....

36 What is the name given to a ship which travels
under water? ....

37 What is the machine called that measures gas
or electricity used? ....

38 What instrument magnifies tiny objects? ....

39 What machine is used in offices to send letters
via the telephone lines? ....
....

40 What instrument held in the hand gives directions? ....

41 What instrument tells if surfaces are level? ....

42 What machine takes photographs through the body? ....

43 What simple instrument is used for drawing straight lines? ....

44 What device will attract iron nails and filings? ....

45 What device tracks aircraft in the sky? ....

Time Test

How many can you write down in the given time?
On a separate sheet of paper make three columns:

Machines   **Instruments**   **Metals**

Write the names you know. Have your list checked.
Count 2 for each correct answer. Check your rating.

Time allowed: 9 and 10 year olds – 2 minutes
11 year olds and over – 1 minute

History

Which kings or queens are connected with the following?

1 Domesday Book.............2   Spanish Armada........3 Magna Carta.................
a William the Conqueror b Queen Elizabeth   c King John

Which kings were known by these nicknames?

4 The Unready .... 5 Coeur-de-Lion .... 6 The Great ....
a Ethelred   b Alfred   c Richard I

Who were the leaders of the following?

7 The Red Shirts ....8 The Lollards............ 9 The Nazis ....
a Hitler   b Garibaldi   c Wycliffe

Who won these victories?

10 Blenheim .... 11 Agincourt .... 12 Borodino ....
a Duke of Marlborough   b King Henry V   c Napoleon

In which years did these Civil Wars begin?

13 American .... 14 Spanish .... 15 English ....
a 1642   b 1936   c 1861

In which wars were these battles fought?

16 Balaclava .... 17 Bosworth Field..... 18 Poitiers ....
a Wars of the Roses   b Hundred Years' War c Crimean War

Who founded the following?

19 The Post Office ....20 The Methodists......... 21 London Police ....
a John Wesley   b Sir Robert Peel   c Sir Rowland Hill

With which kings or queens are these people associated?

22 Thomas Cromwell .... 23 William Cecil .... 24 Benjamin Disraeli ....
a Queen Elizabeth I   b Queen Victoria   c King Henry VIII

With which revolutions are these persons associated?

25 Lenin .... 26 William of Orange .... 27 Robespierre ....
a 'Glorious Revolution'   b French Revolution   c Russian Revolution

Of which countries were these persons active patriots?

28 Churchill .... 29 Bismarck .... 30 Joan of Arc ....
a Germany   b England   c France

31 Where was Napoleon Bonaparte born? ....

32 Who was the British queen who resisted the Romans? ....

33 Where was Alexander the Great born? ....

34 Which English queen was called 'Good'? ....

35 What nickname was given to Cromwell's troops? ....

36 Who was called the 'Führer' in the 1930s? ....

37 Who was murdered in Canterbury Cathedral? ....

38 What was France called when it was part of the
Roman Empire? ....

39 Who was the Roman general who landed in Britain
in 55 and 54 B.C.? ....

40 Who was president during the American Civil War? ....

41 The Lancastrians wore red roses. Who wore white? ....

42 What great city fell to the Turks in 1453? ....

43 Which British monarch lived longest? ....

44 Where are the headquarters of the United Nations? ....

45 Whose landing at Sydney in 1788 is remembered on
Australia Day? ....

Time Test

How many can you write down in the given time?
On a separate sheet of paper make three columns:

Castles   **Cathedrals**   **Kings and Queens**

Write the names you know. Have your list checked.
Count 2 for each correct answer. Check your rating.

Time allowed: 9 and 10 year olds – 2 minutes
11 year olds and over – 1 minute

Medley 3

What sounds are made by the following?

1 little bells .... 2 car brakes .... 3 clocks ....
a tick   b tinkle   c screech

What are the special names given to places where the following are made?

4 beer .... 5 bread .... 6 coins ....
a mint   b bakery   c brewery

What are the names of the places where the following are sold?

7 meat .... 8 medicines .... 9 flowers ....
a chemist   b butchers   c florists

Who were the legendary wives of these famous men?

10 Robin Hood .... 11 King Arthur .... 12 Othello ....
a Guinevere   b Maid Marian   c Desdemona

What countries are associated with the following?

13 springbok .... 14 kangaroo .... 15 kiwi ....
a South Africa   b New Zealand   c Australia

What are known by the following Australian names?

16 dingo .... 17 corroboree .... 18 didgeridoo ....
a social party   b wild dog   c musical instrument

Where do most of the people of these races live?

19 Sikhs .... 20 Cossacks .... 21 Basques ....
a Russia   b Spain   c India

Which signs of the zodiac are associated with the following?

22 fish .... 23 crab .... 24 lion ....
a Leo   b Pisces   c Cancer

What kinds of articles are associated with the following?

25 Stradivarius .... 26 Chippendale .... 27 Constable ....
a furniture   b pictures   c violins

Where are these famous art galleries?

28 Louvre .... 29 Tate .... 30 Hermitage ....
a St Petersburg, Russia   b Paris, France   c London, England

16

31 What is the name of the first month in the calendar year? ....

32 What is the city with the largest population? ....

33 Of what word is 'gym' a shortened form? ....

34 Where was Jesus Christ born? ....

35 Where was Mohammed born? ....

36 What battle was fought at Battle? ....

37 What do silkworms normally feed on? ....

38 What detective was created by Conan Doyle? ....

39 In which religion are cows respected as sacred animals? ....

40 What did the Romans call London? ....

41 What is the main ingredient used to make an omelette? ....

42 Which country's flag shows a maple leaf? ....

43 What is the colour of a Jersey cow? ....

44 What was the name of King Arthur's sword? ....

45 In Parliament what does a successful bill become? ....

Time Test

How many can you write down in the given time?
On a separate sheet of paper make three columns:

Continents   **Breeds of Dog**   **Musical Instruments**

Write the names you know. Have your list checked.
Count 2 for each correct answer. Check your rating.

Time allowed: 9 and 10 year olds – 2 minutes
11 year olds and over – 1 minute

Books and Words

In what kinds of books will you find information about the following?

1 telephone numbers .... 2 maps .... 3 words ....
a dictionary   b atlas   c directory

What kinds of creatures are these animals in stories?

4 Macavity .... 5 Black Beauty .... 6 Mrs Tiggy-Winkle ....
a cat   b hedgehog   c horse

In which books can these villains be found?

7 Long John Silver .... 8 Captain Hook .... 9 Fagin ....
a *Oliver Twist*   b *Peter Pan*   c *Treasure Island*

In which novels are these heroines to be found?

10 Arrietty .... 11 Little Nell .... 12 Jo ....
a *Little Women*   b *Old Curiosity Shop*   c *The Borrowers*

What are these remarkable characters?

13 Stig of the Dump .... 14 The Psammead .... 15 Garfield ....
a cat   b sand-fairy   c caveman

In which books are these unusual characters?

16 Bilbo Baggins .... 17 Aslan .... 18 Mildred ....
a *The Worst Witch*   b *The Hobbit*   c *The Lion, the Witch and the Wardrobe*

Who wrote about these characters?

19 Mole and Toad .... 20 Gulliver .... 21 Mowgli ....
a Rudyard Kipling   b Jonathan Swift   c Kenneth Grahame

Who wrote about the following?

22 Winnie the Pooh .... 23 Paddington Bear ...... 24 Peter Rabbit ....
a Beatrix Potter   b Michael Bond   c A.A.Milne

What kinds of works were written or told by the following?

25 Aesop .... 26 Shakespeare .... 27 Homer ....
a plays   b myths   c fables

Which writers set their books in the following strange places?

28 Narnia .... 29 Wonderland .... 30 Island of Sodor ....
a Rev. W. Audrey   b C.S.Lewis   c Lewis Carroll

31 What are the five vowels? ....

32 What kinds of stories did Hans Andersen write? ....

33 Who went to sea in a 'beautiful pea-green boat'? ....

34 At the Mad Hatter's tea-party who ended up in a pot of tea? ....

35 How many fiddlers did King Cole have? ....

36 What pest did the Pied Piper get rid of? ....

37 In a book by Charles Dickens, who asked for more? ....

38 In *Peter Pan*, what was Captain Hook afraid of? ....

39 In Greek mythology, who was king of the gods? ....

40 How many lines are there in a limerick? ....

41 In *The Famous Five*, what was the name of the dog? ....

42 Who travelled to Lilliput? ....

43 In the story by Roald Dahl, what kind of factory does Charlie Bucket get from Mr Wonka? ....

44 What is the nationality of Asterix, the cartoon character invented by Goscinny and Uderzo? ....

45 Who wrote about 'The Iron Man'? ....

Time Test

How many can you write down in the given time?
On a separate sheet of paper make three columns:

Book Titles   **Authors**   **Story Characters**

Write the names you know. Have your list checked.
Count 2 for each correct answer. Check your rating.

Time allowed: 9 and 10 year olds – 2 minutes
11 year olds and over – 1 minute

Sports and Games

Which countries do these famous soccer teams come from?

1 Juventus .... 2 Ajax .... 3 Real Madrid ....
a Netherlands   b Italy   c Spain

With which games or sports are the following associated?

4 Wimbledon .... 5 Lords .... 6 Le Mans ....
a motor racing   b cricket   c lawn tennis

In what games are these terms used?

7 castling .... 8 huffing .... 9 double twenty ....
a darts   b chess   c draughts

In which sports are these terms used?

10 innings .... 11 love .... 12 relay ....
a athletics   b cricket   c tennis

What are the officials called in the following sports?

13 horse racing .... 14 football .... 15 cricket ....
a umpire   b referee   c steward

In which sports are these trophies awarded?

16 Davis Cup .... 17 Calcutta Cup .... 18 Ryder Cup ....
a golf   b rugby football   c lawn tennis

With what sports or recreations are these clubs connected?

19 Harlem Globe-   20 Royal and   21 Harlequins ....
    Trotters ....   Ancient ....
a rugby football   b basket-ball   c golf

In which sports have these persons gained their fame?

22 Adrian Moorhouse .... 23 Sandy Lyle .... 24 Steffi Graf ....
a swimming   b tennis   c golf

How many persons comprise a team in these sports?

25 field hockey .... 26 netball .... 27 field polo ....
a 7   b 11   c 4

In what countries are these the principal national games?

28 baseball .... 29 ice hockey .... 30 hurling ....
a Irish Republic   b United States   c Canada

31 In what sport might you do a crawl and win? ....

32 How many pieces are there in a game of draughts? ....

33 What game is played on links with clubs? ....

34 In what sport is the 'Yellow Jersey' worn? ....

35 Who plays for the Ashes? ....

36 How many miles are run in the Olympic Marathon? ....

37 In lawn tennis what is an ace? ....

38 How many points does a 'bull' in darts score? ....

39 Who first ran a mile in less than 4 minutes? ....

40 On which river is the famous University Boat Race contested? ....

41 What sport is sometimes described as 'All-In'? ....

42 What is the maximum number of sets in a major men's tennis match? ....

43 In soccer what does a team get if they are awarded a penalty? ....

44 In which sport are Lonsdale belts awarded? ....

45 In a boat race what does the coxswain do? ....

Time Test

How many can you write down in the given time?
On a separate sheet of paper make three columns:

Sports Day Events	**Outdoor Sports played with a ball**	**Indoor Games played on a board**

Write the names you know. Have your list checked.
Count 2 for each correct answer. Check your rating.

Time allowed: 9 and 10 year olds – 2 minutes
                        11 year olds and over – 1 minute

Medley 4

What sounds are made by the following?

1 donkey ....   2 wolf ....   3 pigeon ....
a howls   b coos   c brays

What are the fresh fruits that produce the following?

4 raisins ....   5 prunes ....   6 copra ....
a plums   b coconuts   c grapes

What are the special names given to the following places?

7 burial places ....8 water stores .... 9 car stores ....
a reservoirs   b cemeteries   c garages

What colours are the following shades?

10 ultramarine ....   11 emerald ....   12 scarlet ....
a green   b red   c blue

How many edges and sides have the following?

13 a cone ....   14 a cylinder .... 15 a cube ....
a 2 edges 3 sides   b 1 edge 2 sides   c 8 edges 6 sides

With which countries are the following people associated?

16 gendarmes ....17 mounties ....18 gurkhas ....
a Nepal   b Canada   c France

With which historical characters are the following associated?

19 an oak tree ....20 an apple .... 21 a spider ....
a King Charles II   b Sir Isaac Newton   c Robert the Bruce

What are the main territorial divisions of the following countries?

22 Switzerland ....23 France .... 24 Canada ....
a departments   b provinces   c cantons

With what would you be concerned if you were a member of the following?

25 WHO ....   26 IMF ....   27 UNICEF ....
a children   b finance   c health

What are the simple names of the following pastimes?

28 numismatics ....29 pyrotechnics .... 30 philately ....
a stamp collecting   b coin collecting   c firework displays

31 What colour mixed with blue makes green? ....

32 What does the 'X' in Roman figures stand for? ....

33 What is the chief export of Zambia? ....

34 What name is given to the Friday before Easter Day? ....

35 How many Georges have reigned in Britain altogether? ....

36 Which month is sometimes called the 'Merry Month'? ....

37 What animal may suffer from distemper and rabies? ....

38 In the fairy tale what did the 'Ugly Duckling' grow into? ....

39 Where, in Italy, is the famous leaning tower? ....

40 In Roald Dahl's book, what does B.F.G. stand for? ....

41 On what kind of tree do conkers grow? ....

42 What is the name given to the month of fasting in the Muslim year? ....

43 What is the chief money unit in Canada? ....

44 What mountain range separates Spain and France? ....

45 How often do the Olympic Games take place? ....

Time Test

How many can you write down in the given time?
On a separate sheet of paper make three columns:

Boys' Names   **Occupations**   **Vegetables**

Write the names you know. Have your list checked.
Count 2 for each correct answer. Check your rating.

Time allowed: 9 and 10 year olds – 2 minutes
                  11 year olds and over – 1 minute

Travel

In which countries are these tourist attractions?

1 Pyramids .... 2 Colosseum .... 3 Parthenon ....
   a Greece   b Egypt   c Italy

Which forms of transport are associated with the following?

4 Wright brothers .... 5 Stephenson .... 6 Gottlieb Daimler ....
   a car   b railway train   c aeroplane

Which great men sailed in these ships?

7 Santa Maria .... 8 Endeavour .... 9 Golden Hind ....
   a Sir Francis Drake   b Christopher Columbus c Captain James Cook

In which countries are important roads named the following?

10 freeways .... 11 autostrada .... 12 autobahnen ....
    a USA   b Italy   c Germany

What kinds of vehicles had these famous names?

13 The Rocket .... 14 Cutty Sark .... 15 Nautilus ....
    a clipper ship   b submarine   c locomotive

Who were the famous travellers in these ships?

16 Argo .... 17 Beagle .... 18 Mayflower ....
    a Jason   b Pilgrim Fathers   c Charles Darwin

Which cities are near these?

19 Table Mountain .... 20 Mount Cook .... 21 Mount Fujiyama ....
    a Tokyo   b Cape Town   c Christchurch

In which towns are these railway stations?

22 Gard du Nord .... 23 Grand Central .... 24 Euston ....
    a London   b New York   c Paris

Which cities are served by the following airports?

25 Leonardo da Vinci...... 26 Schipol .... 27 Orly ....
    a Paris   b Rome   c Amsterdam

Which are the foreign ports that stand near the mouths of these rivers?

28 Seine .... 29 Hudson .... 30 St Lawrence ....
    a Montreal   b Le Havre   c New York

31 What is the fuel normally used by cars? ....

32 What was the fuel used for the first railway locomotives? ....

33 Which city divided by a wall allowed its frontier to be opened in 1989? ....

34 What is *Concorde*? ....

35 What are railway sleepers? ....

36 Why do ports have dry docks? ....

37 What Russian vehicle was drawn by 3 horses? ....

38 Where is the Sea of Tranquillity? ....

39 What is the shortest sea crossing between England and France? ..../...............

40 What countries are connected by the Simplon Tunnel? ..../...............

41 In which year did the Channel Tunnel open? ....

42 Of what word is 'bus' a shortened form? ....

43 How long is the Panama Canal: 50 or 500 or 5,000 miles? ....

44 What colour flag means 'infectious sickness on board ship'? ....

45 Which country operates the Qantas Airline? ....

Time Test

How many can you write down in the given time?
On a separate sheet of paper make three columns:

Makes of Cars   **Kinds of Ships**   **Names of Airlines**

Write the names you know. Have your list checked.
Count 2 for each correct answer. Check your rating.

Time allowed: 9 and 10 year olds – 2 minutes
                  11 year olds and over – 1 minute

Geography

In which countries are these cities?

1 Glasgow .... 2 Manchester .... 3 Melbourne ....
a England   b Australia   c Scotland

Of which countries are these the capital cities?

4 Paris .... 5 Madrid .... 6 Delhi ....
a Spain   b France   c India

In which continents are these ranges of mountains?

7 Andes .... 8 Atlas .... 9 Alps ....
a Europe   b South America   c Africa

In which mountain ranges are these peaks?

10 Mount Everest .... 11 Matterhorn .... 12 Mount Logan ....
a Rocky Mountains   b Himalayas   c Alps

On which rivers do these towns stand?

13 Dublin .... 14 Vienna .... 15 Cologne ....
a Danube   b Rhine   c Liffey

What are the national emblems of these countries?

16 Ireland .... 17 Scotland .... 18 Wales ....
a leek   b thistle   c shamrock

In which countries do or did these people live?

19 Bretons .... 20 Maori .... 21 Aborigines ....
a Australia   b France   c New Zealand

In which countries are these money units used?

22 lira .... 23 rouble .... 24 rupee ....
a Italy   b India   c Russia

In which groups of islands will these islands be found?

25 Jersey .... 26 Jamaica .... 27 Majorca ....
a Caribbean   b Balearic   c Channel

In what cities are these special places to be found?

28 Kremlin .... 29 Vatican .... 30 Eiffel Tower ....
a Rome (Italy)   b Moscow (Russia)   c Paris (France)

31 What is the highest mountain in the world? ....

32 Which country produces the most coffee? ....

33 Into which ocean does the river Amazon flow? ....

34 In which country is Mount Popocatepetl? ....

35 How did the Dead Sea get its name? ....

36 What country is known as the 'Emerald Isle'? ....

37 What country has two main islands, one called North and the other called South? ....

38 On which river is the Aswan High Dam? ....

39 What is the sacred river of the Hindus? ....

40 Which Australian state has the largest population? ....

41 On which island do Manx people live? ....

42 What is the largest island in the world? ....

43 Which is the largest of Japan's many islands? ....

44 What is the Sahara? ....

45 In Australia, is 'Alice Springs' a river, town or mountain? ....

Time Test

How many can you write down in the given time?
On a separate sheet of paper make three columns:

Towns   **Countries**   **Rivers**

Write the names you know. Have your list checked.
Count 2 for each correct answer. Check your rating.

Time allowed: 9 and 10 year olds – 2 minutes
                   11 year olds and over – 1 minute

Nature

How many legs do these creatures have?

1 spider .... 2 fly .... 3 tiger ....
a four b eight c six

Name the parents of these young creatures

4 chicken .... 5 puppy .... 6 kitten ....
a hen b dog c cat

Give the names of the young of these creatures

7 horse .... 8 sheep .... 9 goat ....
a kid b foal c lamb

What names are given to the homes of these animals?

10 dog .... 11 rabbit .... 12 horse ....
a stable b hutch c kennel

What do we call a group of the following?

13 cattle .... 14 sheep .... 15 puppies ....
a litter b flock c herd

Give the names of the young of these creatures

16 cow .... 17 leopard .... 18 salmon ....
a cub b calf c parr

What names are given to the homes of these creatures?

19 badger .... 20 hare .... 21 fox ....
a sett b earth c form

What do we call a group of the following?

22 lions .... 23 wolves .... 24 whales ....
a pack b school c pride

What do we call the females of these males?

25 boar .... 26 buck .... 27 gander ....
a sow b goose c doe

What things in nature suffer from these pests or diseases?

28 foot and mouth .... 29 Colorado beetle .... 30 swine fever ....
a pigs b potatoes c cattle

31 Where does the kangaroo carry its young? ....

32 What small creature spins a web to catch its prey? ....

33 In what part of its body does the camel store its fat? ....

34 What large animal uses a trunk to drink water? ....

35 What is the bird with a familiar call that does not build a nest? ....

36 What is the animal with the longest neck? ....

37 What is the largest bird in the world? ....

38 What member of the cat family is the fastest animal over short distances? ....

39 What is the natural home of the otter? ....

40 What is the smallest bird in the world? ....

41 What flower has a name which means 'lion's tooth'? ....

42 Which insect with the same name as a game sings and lives near fires? ....

43 What name is given to a fox's tail? ....

44 What bird has a call 'too-whit, too-whoo', and is heard at night? ....

45 What animal is proverbial for changing its colour? ....

Time Test

How many can you write down in the given time?
On a separate sheet of paper make three columns:

Animals   **Birds**   **Flowers and Trees**

Write the names you know. Have your list checked.
Count 2 for each correct answer. Check your rating.

Time allowed: 9 and 10 year olds – 2 minutes
                  11 year olds and over – 1 minute

Answers

Page 4. Medley 1

1c, 2b, 3a: 4b, 5c, 6a: 7b, 8a, 9c: 10c, 11b, 12a: 13b, 14a, 15c: 16c, 17a, 18b:
19c, 20b, 21a: 22a, 23c, 24b: 25a, 26c, 27b: 28b, 29c, 30a:

31 lean   32 yolk   33 H.M.S. Victory   34 whey   35 in the tail   36 oak
37 grandfather   38 King Arthur's   39 rose   40 Beefeaters   41 8   42 elbow
43 7   44 52 +2 jokers   45 100

Page 6. People

1b, 2c, 3a: 4c, 5a, 6b: 7c, 8b, 9a: 10a, 11c, 12b: 13c, 14a, 15b: 16c, 17b, 18a:
19b, 20a, 21c: 22b, 23c, 24a: 25b, 26a, 27c: 28b, 29c, 30a

31 Egypt   32 Judas   33 Mohammed   34 Sir Walter Raleigh   35 Kaiser
36 Ronald Reagan   37 Gorbachev   38 Leo Tolstoy   39 Valentina Tereshkova
40 Betty Boothroyd   41 Christiaan Barnard   42 Australia
43 Margaret Thatcher   44 King George VI   45 Chairman Mao Tse-tung

Page 8. Food and Drink

1b, 2c, 3a: 4c, 5a, 6b: 7a, 8c, 9b: 10b, 11c, 12a: 13b, 14c, 15a: 16a, 17b, 18c:
19c, 20b, 21a: 22b, 23c, 24a: 25c, 26a, 27b: 28a, 29c, 30b

31 rice   32 fish   33 herring   34 mint   35 choux pastry   36 cocoa/chocolate
37 oranges   38 oatmeal   39 beef   40 bee   41 tea   42 milk   43 bramble
44 milk   45 seeds

Page 10. Medley 2

1b, 2a, 3c: 4b, 5c, 6a: 7b, 8c, 9a: 10c, 11a, 12b: 13a, 14c, 15b: 16b, 17c, 18a:
19b, 20c, 21a: 22c, 23b, 24a: 25b, 26c, 27a: 28c, 29a, 30b

31 refrigerator   32 Nile   33 Robin Hood   34 10   35 Budapest   36 6
37 lariat/lassoo   38 chiropodist   39 blue   40 blue   41 Madame Tussaud
42 blue   43 sea-bird   44 volcanoes   45 Finland

Page 12. Science and Machines

1b, 2c, 3a: 4b, 5c, 6a: 7a, 8c, 9b: 10c, 11a, 12b: 13b, 14a, 15c: 16a, 17b, 18c:
19b, 20c, 21a: 22b, 23a, 24c: 25b, 26a, 27c: 28c, 29a, 30b

31 carbon   32 100°   33 0°   34 camera   35 time   36 submarine   37 meter
38 microscope   39 fax machine   40 compass   41 spirit-level   42 X-rays
43 ruler   44 magnet   45 radar

Page 14. History

1a, 2b, 3c: 4a, 5c, 6b: 7b, 8c, 9a: 10a, 11b, 12c: 13c, 14b, 15a: 16c, 17a, 18b:
19c, 20a, 21b: 22c, 23a, 24b: 25c, 26a, 27b: 28b, 29a, 30c

31 Corsica   32 Boadicea or Boudicca   33 Macedonia, Greece   34 Elizabeth I
(Bess)   35 Ironsides   36 Adolf Hitler   37 Thomas à Becket   38 Gaul
39 Julius Caesar   40 Abraham Lincoln   41 Yorkists   42 Constantinople

Page 16. Medley 3

1b, 2c, 3a: 4c, 5b, 6a: 7b, 8a, 9c: 10b, 11a, 12c: 13a, 14c, 15b: 16b, 17a, 18c:
19c, 20a, 21b: 22b, 23c, 24a: 25c, 26a, 27b: 28b, 29c, 30a

31 January   32 Mexico City   33 gymnasium   34 Bethlehem   35 Mecca   36
Hastings   37 mulberry leaves   38 Sherlock Holmes   39 Hinduism
40 Londinium   41 egg   42 Canada   43 light brown   44 Excalibur   45 act/law

Page 18. Books and Words

1c, 2b, 3a: 4a, 5c, 6b: 7c, 8b, 9a: 10c, 11b, 12a: 13c, 14b, 15a: 16b, 17c, 18a:
19c, 20b, 21a: 22c, 23b, 24a: 25c, 26a, 27b: 28b, 29c, 30a

31 a-e-i-o-u   32 fairy tales   33 Owl and Pussy-cat   34 Dormouse   35 3
36 rats   37 Oliver Twist   38 crocodile   39 Zeus   40 5   41 Timmy
42 Gulliver   43 chocolate   44 Gallic   45 Ted Hughes

Page 20. Sports and Games

1b, 2a, 3c: 4c, 5b, 6a: 7b, 8c, 9a: 10b, 11c, 12a: 13c, 14b, 15a: 16c, 17b, 18a:
19b, 20c, 21a: 22a, 23c, 24b: 25b, 26a, 27c: 28b, 29c, 30a

31 swimming   32 24   33 golf   34 cycling   35 England v. Australia cricket XIs
36 26   37 an unplayable serve   38 50   39 Roger Bannister   40 Thames
41 wrestling   42 5   43 free kick at goal   44 boxing   45 steer

Page 22. Medley 4

1c, 2a, 3b: 4c, 5a, 6b: 7b, 8a, 9c: 10c, 11a, 12b: 13b, 14a, 15c: 16c, 17b, 18a:
19a, 20b, 21c: 22c, 23a, 24b: 25c, 26b, 27a: 28b, 29c, 30a

31 yellow   32 ten   33 copper   34 Good Friday   35 6   36 May   37 dog
38 swan   39 Pisa   40 Big Friendly Giant   41 horse chestnut   42 Ramadan
43 dollar   44 Pyrenees   45 every four years

Page 24. Travel

1b, 2c, 3a: 4c, 5b, 6a: 7b, 8c, 9a: 10a, 11b, 12c: 13c, 14a, 15b: 16a, 17c, 18b:
19b, 20c, 21a: 22c, 23b, 24a: 25b, 26c, 27a: 28b, 29c, 30a
31 petrol   32 coal   33 Berlin   34 supersonic aircraft
35 supports for railway lines   36 to carry out maintenance   37 troika
38 on the moon   39 Dover/Calais   40 Switzerland/Italy   41 1994
42 omnibus   43 50 miles   44 yellow   45 Australia

Page 26. Geography

1c, 2a, 3b: 4b, 5a, 6c: 7b, 8c, 9a: 10b, 11c, 12a: 13c, 14a, 15b: 16c, 17b, 18a:
19b, 20c, 21a: 22a, 23c, 24b: 25c, 26a, 27b: 28b, 29a, 30c
31 Mount Everest   32 Brazil   33 Atlantic Ocean   34 Mexico
35 the salt in the sea kills living things   36 Ireland   37 New Zealand
38 Nile   39 Ganges   40 New South Wales   41 Isle of Man   42 Australia
43 Honshu   44 desert   45 a town

Page 28. Nature

1b, 2c, 3a: 4a, 5b, 6c: 7b, 8c, 9a: 10c, 11b, 12a: 13c, 14b, 15a: 16b, 17a, 18c:
19a, 20c, 21b: 22c, 23a, 24b: 25a, 26c, 27b: 28c, 29b, 30a
31 in a pouch   32 spider   33 in its hump   34 elephant   35 cuckoo   36 giraffe
37 ostrich   38 cheetah   39 river   40 humming bird   41 dandelion   42 cricket
43 brush   44 owl   45 chameleon

Rating Chart

Score 1 point for each question you have answered correctly.
Score 2 points for each correct answer in a Time Test.
Add up the total number of points you have scored, and check your star
rating for each section.

	*	* *	* * *
Age 9	20 – 30	32 – 40	42+
Age 10	20 – 30	32 – 50	52+
Age 11+	20 – 30	32 – 60	62+